Successful Selling
In A Week

Christine Harvey

D1448659

The Teach Yourself series has been trusted around the world
for over 60 years. This series of 'In A Week' business books is
designed to help people at all levels and around the world to
further their careers. Learn, in a week, what the experts learn
in a lifetime.

H46 320 773 7

Christine Harvey and her organization have trained thousands of people across Europe, America and Asia. Whether selling products, services or concepts, she is called upon by the British and Australian Institutes of Management, the US Military and corporations worldwide to help individuals and organizations raise sales and performance levels. She is the author of six books published in 28 languages. These include *Successful People Skills In A Week*, *Your Pursuit of Profit*, *Public Speaking & Leadership Building*, *Can a Girl Run for President?* and *Secrets of the World's Top Sales Performers*, an international best-seller.

Teach® Yourself

Successful Selling

Christine Harvey

www.inaweek.co.uk

Hodder Education

338 Euston Road, London NW1 3BH.

Hodder Education is an Hachette UK company

First published in UK 1992 by Hodder Education

This edition published 2012.

www.hoddereducation.co.uk

Typeset by Cenveo Publisher Services.

Printed and bound by CPI Group (UK) Ltd, Croydon, CR0 4YY.

Contents

Introduction

The idea of selling as an occupation leaves many people terror-stricken, and yet selling is an integral part of running any business. Good salespeople are in great demand. Sales skills are essential in starting any business, and successful selling brings with it career progression, satisfaction and personal growth that are second to none.

With this book, you'll learn *all* the components necessary to become *not just a good but a great salesperson*. Whether you're new to sales, and want to start out with a bang, or a veteran salesperson who wants to maximize results, *Successful Selling In A Week* will be a huge asset to you now and in years to come.

You'll learn ways to increase the effectiveness of your efforts, save time and energy and get the best results possible, regardless of your field of sales. You'll be able to put together your own system of success, just like the people before you from whom these principles are drawn. Successful selling means using a structured set of systems that all professional high achievers can learn. We will look at each of these steps one day at a time.

You may be wondering if your personality is right for sales. You may think that it's important to be a good talker, but it's far more important to be a sincere listener, to be able to ask pertinent questions leading to buying motives, and then be able to present the features and benefits of your product or service as they *match* your customer's needs. A person who does all the talking, without the right questioning and listening, will be wasting time and effort.

There is, in fact, no one right personality for sales. Most of us can use the skills we've developed over our lifetime, and hone them with the principles of this book to become a top-notch, if not world-class, salesperson.

I've spent much of my life selling, training salespeople, and writing about those top-notch sales skills. In another of my books, *Secrets of the World's Top Sales Performers*, I interviewed ten of the world's top salespeople in ten countries and ten industries. The one secret of success they all shared was consistency. They each had their own system and they used it day in and day out.

The same will be true for you. You'll be able to use the techniques in this book to design sales skills that work best for you, your personality and your industry. So dig in and enjoy. I wish you success in your journey, every step of the way.

It would be my greatest pleasure to hear how you applied the material. Writing a book is like giving birth to an offspring, taking about nine months to develop after years of personal growth. As our children grow to be teens and adults, it's nice to hear great stories about them. So, if you have questions or stories to tell me – or you wish to enquire about our seminars – you can reach me at ChristineHarvey@ChristineHarvey.com, or via the publishers.

Wishing you all the best,

Christine Harvey

SUNDAY

Jump-start your success formula

I have often travelled to Hong Kong and Singapore, where business competition is fierce. A journalist there asked me about the principles of my books and courses. 'Mrs Harvey, why are you so adamant about targets for salespeople? Isn't it enough just to do your best?'

'Well, look at it like this,' I responded. 'If you were training to be an Olympic champion runner, would you go out every day and practise running any distance at any speed, just doing your best? Or would you know exactly how far you had to run, and at what speed, in order to meet your defined goal?'

'Oh, yes, I see,' she responded. That made sense to her. It's painful for people to work hard and do their best, to have high expectations and then be let down.

Today you will learn how to set and achieve goals that are *right for you*. You won't fail by thinking sales will come to you magically, or later if you wait. Instead, you'll be planning your best formula for success. You will learn how to:

- adopt new methods of operation
- set your overall goal
- create daily targets
- measure your results
- carry out the actions needed for success.

Adopt new methods of operation

Do you remember the last time you changed jobs? Did it require a mental adjustment of your self-image? The chances are that you needed time to grow into the new shoes.

I remember sitting on a plane from London, bound for Chicago, to meet my first prospective client after I started my company. I still felt allegiance to my old company, my old job and my old colleagues because I had no experiences to draw upon for my new role. If you are just starting out in sales, or changing companies, you may experience this too.

However, psychologists say that we can do a lot for ourselves to speed up the acclimatization process. If we visualize ourselves working in the new role, feeling comfortable in the new role and succeeding in the new role, we will acclimatize faster.

Whether we are new to sales or want to improve our returns, we'll be adopting new methods of operation. We'll be forcing ourselves in new directions, putting ourselves under new pressures, disciplining ourselves and setting new goals. All of these will require that we see ourselves differently. The sooner we do this, the sooner we'll succeed.

Let's look at the specific areas in which you'll want to see yourself operating successfully as preparation for selling.

Preparing for success

- Set your overall goal.
- Break the goal into daily work segments.
- Carry out these daily segments.
- Gain prospective customers.
- Spend time on critical activities.
- Create self-management system charts.
- Organize work systems.

Set your overall goal

Start at the top of the list and set your goals. What do you want to achieve? Calculate it in some specific terms. Will it be a monetary figure, a percentage or multiple of a target set by your company, a possession to be acquired, or even a promotion?

Now think about how to convert that goal to the actual number of sales you need in order to achieve your target. Good. Now the next step is critical and this is the step most unsuccessful salespeople avoid. Divide your total sales into weekly and daily sales and then calculate the work necessary to achieve that.

Calculate workload

Ask yourself the following questions about workload.

- How many sales do I want?
- How many prospects will I need to see in order to make one sale?
- How many prospects do I need in order to reach my total sales target?
- How many activities do I need to do to generate one prospect?
  - Telephone calls
  - Direct mail or emailed letters

- Exhibitions or seminars
- Advertisements
- Cold calling
- Other

● What daily activity schedule and results do I have to maintain in order to achieve my goal? (Include visits, telephone calls and all of the above.)

Self-deception

Bob Adams, one of the world's top insurance salesmen, puts it in strong terms. He says that the single biggest failure salespeople make is *self-deception*. He said he wasn't 'born with success'. He had to study the most successful sales people he could find.

His advice? 'Don't fool yourself into thinking you're selling when you're sitting at your desk. If you're not in front of the right number of people every day, working eight hours per day is not the point. It's what you do in those eight hours that counts.'

If you're not in front of enough prospects, you won't sell enough to make your target. And how do you get in front of

SUNDAY

MONDAY

TUESDAY

WEDNESDAY

THURSDAY

FRIDAY

SATURDAY

enough prospects? By making enough appointments. It's that straightforward. 'Yet many people fool themselves thinking they are selling when in fact they are doing busy work,' says Bob.

> *Often, the difference between success and failure is neglecting to break down your overall goal into daily targets and tasks.*

Let's look at advice from people who succeed year after year. How do they put this principle into practice?

One salesman with a worldwide reputation for success is Ove from Sweden. He has calculated his yearly target and broken it down into a daily figure. He knows exactly how many sales he must make per day. He knows how many prospects he must see each day.

He stresses that staying at the top is easy if you know how much you must do every day and you do it.

Not me!

'Oh, daily targets don't relate to me,' many people argue. That's the biggest misconception I hear from our seminar delegates. They really believe they can't break *their* activity into daily targets. This is the first mental change we must *all* make if we are to succeed in selling.

> *Sales come about from methodically carrying out the right practices, day in and day out.*

Whether we sell large systems to governments that require three years to close, consulting projects that take a year to close or retail products to customers that take three minutes to close, we still have to calculate *which* daily component parts will lead us to success. Even if we only want three customers per year, we'll have to be negotiating with six, nine or twelve prospects constantly. We need to know *how many* and keep this running *constantly*.

In the interviews I undertook for my book *Secrets of the World's Top Sales Performers*, I found that every single top sales performer in every industry knows their daily sales target and daily activity schedule. Did their companies tell them? No. They've calculated it themselves. It's exactly what we all must do if we want true and lasting success.

TIP *You must know your daily targets for finding prospects and do that first. That means making appointments and seeing prospects. Everything else is secondary.*

Create daily targets

Why do we put so much emphasis on daily sales targets and daily activity targets? It's because we've seen so many failures by talented, hard-working, well-meaning people who deserved to succeed. No one ever sat them down and said, 'Look, success comes by doing the right number of activities day in and day out.'

Make reminders

We know that you are reading this book in order to succeed. You want to use a strategic approach. You want to avoid the pitfalls of others. Therefore, take today to plan your targets. Plan the systems you will use for reaching your targets.

Create prompts on wall charts, screen savers and pocket memos – anything and everything you need to remind yourself that hard work alone will not bring you success. It's a matter of scheduling and seeing the right number of people today as well as carrying out specific activities that will allow you to see the right number of people tomorrow.

Calculate the numbers

What is the right number? If we need one sale per day and we have to see three prospects in order to convert one to a sale, then we need three sales visits per day. That's if we can do one-call closings; in other words, if we need to see each prospect only once. But what if we need to see each prospect twice on average and we need to make one sale per day? How many sales visits will we need to do every day? Six.

We'll need time for making appointments and time for following up on promises we make during the appointments. It's therefore essential to plan our targets and break them into daily workloads.

Pitfalls for business owners too

New business owners have exactly the same problem, and we can learn from them. Here's an example. Two talented young dress designers with their own shop asked me for advice on succeeding in their business. They had many loyal customers but they were afraid they wouldn't make enough money to stay in business.

Here are the questions that they needed to ask themselves.

- How much money do we need to make?
- What are our expenses?
- How many do we need to sell per year to cover all our expenses and leave us with a profit?
- How many is that per week?
- What do we need to do in order to sell that many each week?

They hadn't thought about it that way. They were just going to do the best they could. Were they unusual? No. That's the naïve approach you want to avoid, regardless of your industry.

Are 'good products' enough?

I was fortunate to work with a British enterprise agency launched by Prince Charles that helps people start new businesses. Through that experience of working on the Board, I saw hundreds of people who thought it was enough to have a 'good product' and 'do their best'. Yet, as time went on, those who succeeded learned that they had to know *exactly* what their sales targets were every week and every day. Then they had to focus all their energy on making sure those targets were met, to ensure that they didn't go out of business.

Selling helps you succeed

You don't want to be out of business or out of the sales business. There are tremendous opportunities in sales, including:

- opportunities for self-development
- opportunities for promotion
- opportunities for helping people
- job satisfaction
- financial wealth
- progression towards running your own business if that's what you want.

However, few business owners today succeed without strong emphasis and skills on the sales side. Likewise, few people today in the corporate world progress without being able to sell their ideas.

Millions of people are involved in the production of products or services. All their jobs rely on people being able to sell those products or services. Corporations need you.

TIP

The economies of the world rely on continued sales. Your skills and your success are more important than you realize.

Measure your results

Whatever your goal, start by measuring your targets and breaking them into daily segments and tasks. Remember that today is your day of preparation and your success later will mainly depend on your plan and your dedication to your plan. The following chart shows the most critical factors to measure, i.e. the number of sales visits (target and actual) and the number of sales (target and actual).

Self-management wall chart and computer graph

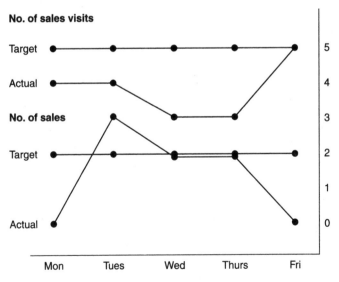

Predicting shortfalls

If your wall chart and computer graph show you that your actual sales *visits* are 25 per cent below your target for one week, you can expect to be 25 per cent down on sales unless you make up that number of visits the following week.

Sales do not come about magically, and that's what your management control wall charts and computer graphs remind you instantly.

Actions for success

Will you reach the success level you hope for? Selling is not a mystical process. It's a predictable, logical, step-by-step process like a production line. When we put in the right component parts, we get the correct end product. When we put in fewer component parts than necessary, we get an inferior end product. There is no mystery about salesmanship.

Much of your success will depend on coming to terms with the actual component parts of salesmanship.

Planning our success by setting our daily workload is the first component part. Over the next six days you will learn about the other component parts. When we carry out each component part in the right quantity, with the right quality and frequency, we have success.

Our results come from our actions, not from our understanding. It's said that 'Knowledge without action serves no one.' This is never truer than in sales. Pick up your pen and start *now* to create your targets *and* your self-management system charts. Success is in your hands.

SUNDAY

MONDAY

TUESDAY

WEDNESDAY

THURSDAY

FRIDAY

SATURDAY

Summary

Today we talked about the importance of targets. We started with the overall goal – for example, an annual income goal. We tied that to the number of products or services we need to sell, then broke that down further into weekly and daily sales targets.

We then looked at the *activity* needed to accomplish those goals. This means the number of prospects needed to gain one sale, and the number of phone calls or marketing campaigns needed to gain one prospect.

Just as $2 + 2 = 4$, we saw that, without the right number of actions each day, be it phone calls, visits or marketing pieces – and probably all of these – we can't possibly reach our goal. How much better it is to know this in advance, because then we can change our strategy and systems, or even our targets.

As one of the world's top salespeople says, 'Don't let self-deception be your enemy!' We have to know how to break down targets and set our daily activity level in advance in order to become the top achiever we wish to be. Start now. Go for it, and enjoy!

Remember
Knowledge without action serves no one

SUNDAY

MONDAY

TUESDAY

WEDNESDAY

THURSDAY

FRIDAY

SATURDAY

Fact-check (answers at the back)

1. What does changing careers or improving results in your current sales position require?
   a) Mental adjustment of your self-image ❏
   b) Visualizing yourself working in a new role ❏
   c) Visualizing feeling comfortable in the new role and succeeding in the new role ❏
   d) All of the above ❏

2. What can setting goals successfully mean?
   a) Calculating a monetary figure ❏
   b) Targeting a possession to be acquired ❏
   c) Aiming for a promotion ❏
   d) All of the above ❏

3. After deciding on your goal, what should your first step be?
   a) To tell your best friend and ask for support ❏
   b) To convert your goal to the actual number of sales you need in order to achieve your target ❏
   c) To discuss the practicality of your goal with your boss ❏
   d) To celebrate ❏

4. After dividing their annual sales goal into weekly and daily sales targets, what do most unsuccessful salespeople avoid doing?
   a) Writing it down ❏
   b) Entering the data into their computer ❏
   c) Calculating the work necessary to achieve that goal ❏
   d) Telling anyone ❏

5. What is the single biggest failure of most salespeople?
   a) Talking too much at the first meeting ❏
   b) Self-deception ❏
   c) Being rude to the customer ❏
   d) Giving their boss false hope ❏

6. In order to know how many prospects to see each day, what must you know?
   a) How many sales you want ❏
   b) How many prospects you need to make one sale ❏
   c) How many activities you need to do to generate one prospect ❏
   d) All of the above ❏

7. Why do most unsuccessful salespeople and business owners avoid using goals and targets?
a) They firmly believe that doing their best is enough to make them succeed ❑
b) They have never used them before ❑
c) They are afraid to fail ❑
d) They think it is a waste of time ❑

8. A salesman named Sam calculates that he needs one sale per day. On average, one prospect out of three will buy his products, and he normally has to visit each prospect twice before he gets a 'yes' or a 'no'. How many total visits does Sam need to make each day to reach his goal of one sale per day?
a) Two ❑
b) Four ❑
c) Six ❑
d) Eight ❑

9. Why are your skills and success in selling so important?
a) Your livelihood depends on it ❑
b) The economies of the world rely on continued sales ❑
c) The livelihood of your company relies on it ❑
d) All of the above ❑

10. What is the *most* important thing about comparing your actual sales to your targets on a wall chart?
a) You will see at a glance where you stand ❑
b) You can catch up tomorrow if you fall behind today ❑
c) You will gain recognition from your manager and your peers ❑
d) You will keep your morale up ❑

MONDAY

Develop product and service expertise

On one exciting day in my early sales career, I took the company's technical expert out on a sales call with me. She and I were a knockout team. I was expert at asking questions about needs, and she had answers to every conceivable question the customer had about our products and services. Later, when I had my own company, I enjoyed taking my own sales employees out on calls with me and supplying that same knowledge.

The importance of learning from technical people is obvious. They have years of 'behind-the-scenes' experiences from which to draw. And when you become an expert yourself and model the sale process for a newer member of staff, you also gain. You're on your toes. You do things right, knowing that they are watching and learning from you.

There are dozens of ways to gain the product and service knowledge you need to sell well, and one of them is bound to suit your style and interests.

Today you will create your own plan for developing your expertise. You will:

- understand the 'rule of 40'
- find sources of knowledge
- plan your personal strategy.

Understand the 'rule of 40'

Let's start at the beginning. How much knowledge do you need? Perhaps this idea will help you. Dale Carnegie advised his students of public speaking, 'Learn 40 times as much as you will use.'

Why 40 times? It's because our store of information is like a fully charged battery. It shows in our enthusiasm, our self-confidence and most of all in our *competence*. Certainly that's true of selling too.

Let's stop for a moment and think of our customers. How do they view us? Aren't we the only link between the manufactured product or service and themselves? They have to rely on us to tell them *each and every thing* that they might need to know.

It makes sense, then, to have a 40-fold store of knowledge in reserve for every eventuality, over and above what we might use in a single sales discussion with a single customer. Therefore, we need to focus on getting as much knowledge as we can, as quickly as possible.

Invest in yourself

First, let's set the ground rules and clear any misconceptions. In order to reach the top with the desired level of expertise, we should consider the following two principles.

● Expect to invest in ourselves.
● Don't expect the company to provide all our training.

How many years do doctors, lawyers or accountants spend in preparing themselves for their profession? If we want to become experts, we first have to realize that we must invest in ourselves. We have to develop our own plan. If our company trains us, fine. But we cannot use the lack of training as an excuse to hold us back. Success is in our own hands.

'An investment in knowledge pays the best interest.'

Benjamin Franklin

Find sources of knowledge

Where do we start? We want to set a schedule for absorbing our 40-fold expertise in the shortest possible time. There are many effective options, as shown in the box below.

Dynamic sources of product expertise

- Interview current customers.
- Study product literature.
- Study service literature.
- Study operations manuals.
- Take technicians on sales visits.
- Accompany other sales professionals on sales visits.
- Have discussions with operations people, managers, product developers and distributors.
- Observe the production line.
- Utilize web-based training.
- Take training courses of all kinds.

Interview current customers

Interviewing current customers is one of the most valuable yet least exploited options for salespeople. Customers give us the information from the *user's* point of view, which is invaluable.

The customer doesn't want to know, for example, that a fax machine has 'group 3, high-speed, digital transmission technology'. They only want to know that their document can reach their colleague in Australia in six seconds *because* of this group 3, high-speed technology.

We must always stress the benefit, using the technology as proof that the benefit exists.

Why else are we so bullish when we visit or talk to current customers? Because they are a bottomless pit of testimonials, references, new business, add-on business, referrals, inspiration, enthusiasm, and information about competitors. Moreover, they can supply quotable stories, even material for press releases and feature stories. But the most important part is your instant education.

Here is an example. Some years ago I was involved in selling a computer service. Because everyone on the sales team was hired from other industries, we each needed to get

computer training as quickly as possible. I therefore arranged
to accompany a technician on a troubleshooting call. After
she had sorted out the problem, I asked the client a question:
'What made you choose our system over the competitor's?'

'It's so fast to use and error free,' he said. 'We previously
agonized over errors in our systems. Now we complete input
forms every morning. It takes half an hour, maximum. Then
the results come back – perfect, no aggravation.'

That was a testimonial I could use to emphasize speed and
accuracy. It gave our sales team a valuable reference letter
and later we turned it into a press release, which gave it
added value.

The benefits of interviewing customers

The benefits of interviewing our current customers are
many and include the following.

- Through interviews we gain confidence in our product
and company.
- We learn the benefits to the user.
- We build a rapport, which can later lead to further
business.
- We acquire testimonial stories about how the service
is used.
- We gain confidence and inspiration.

We can then repeat the interviewing process with different
industry group users until we have the knowledge we need.
The time it takes will be well worth while.

Plan your personal strategy

Use today to plan your personal strategy for building your
product/service expertise. The following checklist will help you
decide which methods to apply. Who will you go to in order to

get the information? How much time will you allocate to each method? When will you do it? Make a copy of the list and fill it in to create your personal action strategy.

Set up your system today. You may want to call one or two current customers to set up appointments for interviews. You may even want to have the discussion by telephone today, if appropriate. Naturally, it's always better to do it in person if possible. Distances, time and products will dictate the best approach.

TIP

Be sure to allocate enough time every day to update your knowledge.

Creative options for developing product/service expertise

Method	Yes/No	Who	How long	When
1 Interview current customers				
2 Study product literature				
3 Study service literature				
4 Study operations manuals				
5 Take technicians on sales visits				
6 Accompany other sales professionals on sales visits				
7 Have discussions • with operations people • with managers • with product development people • with distributors				
8 Observe the production line				
9 Utilize web-based training				
10 Take training courses				

Look again at your strategy. You may want to spend an hour a day next week reading technical literature, or perhaps two hours today. You may want to invite a technical person to accompany you on your next sales visit, or arrange to accompany them on a technical visit. Decide now, and allocate time in your diary.

Commit to training courses

You may want to persuade your manager that he or she should fund a training course for you from their budget. If you do, be prepared to 'sell' your idea, explaining the benefits the company will get from your enhanced skills. Remember, your boss may have to sell the idea up the line.

But remember the bottom line – your commitment to your own training. If the manager's answer is no, you may have to invest in yourself. Be prepared to take responsibility for your own success.

Professionals spend time and money preparing for success in their career, and selling is as demanding and challenging as any career.

What steps can you take to find training courses that will be valuable to you?

Learn at every appointment

One top sales manager I knew summed it up well when he advised, 'The day you stop learning in sales is the day your professionalism dies.'

After every sales call with any of his sales staff, whether they were new to sales or experienced, he always said, 'Tell me two new things you learned from that visit.' That's good advice for all of us.

> ## Implement your strategy
> Take time now to look back over the options for developing product and service expertise. Decide which options are right for you. Then draw up a segmented strategy of how much time to devote to each option. Take today to plan those segments.

Summary

Today we looked at the many ways we can develop the product and service expertise critical to reaching our sales goals. We touched on the importance of relating the benefits of the products and services to the customer. We learned that, just as in other professions, gaining the training we need is up to us if we want to be among the highest achievers and therefore the highest income earners.

We also saw interesting benefits of designing our own training. For example, if we decide to interview past or current clients, we not only learn what benefits they derive but may also gain testimonials, referrals and even new business from them.

In addition, we might choose to discuss product features with operations, technical and product development people, who can give us valuable contacts as well as knowledge.

Finally, with personal learning in mind we looked at how to plan our strategy, using a personal planning chart for easy implementation.

Remember

The day you stop learning is the day your professionalism dies and your income diminishes.

SUNDAY
MONDAY
TUESDAY
WEDNESDAY
THURSDAY
FRIDAY
SATURDAY

Fact-check (answers at the back)

1. When gaining product and service expertise, how much should you learn?
   a) Twice as much as you might need ☐
   b) Ten times as much as you might need ☐
   c) 40 times as much as you might need ☐
   d) 100 times as much as you might need ☐

2. How do prospective customers normally view us?
   a) The only link between the product or service and themselves ☐
   b) Experts in our field ☐
   c) Untrustworthy ☐
   d) Reliable ☐

3. Who is responsible for the training you receive about the products and services you sell?
   a) The training department ☐
   b) Your boss ☐
   c) You ☐
   d) It depends on the company ☐

4. In which profession is investing in your own education and training considered normal?
   a) The legal profession ☐
   b) The accounting profession ☐
   c) The sales profession ☐
   d) All of the above ☐

5. What is a great way to get training?
   a) Interviewing current customers about the benefits they receive ☐
   b) Studying product and service literature and manuals ☐
   c) Taking training courses of all kinds ☐
   d) All of the above ☐

6. What is one of the most valuable yet least utilized options for training oneself?
   a) Interviewing current customers ☐
   b) Reading manuals ☐
   c) Web-based training ☐
   d) Staying late to study ☐

7. What are the extra benefits of visiting or talking to current customers?
   a) They are a source of testimonials ☐
   b) They often give referrals ☐
   c) They give you inspiration and enthusiasm ☐
   d) All of the above ☐

8. What is a good question to ask a current user when interviewing them?
   a) What do you not like about our product or service? ☐
   b) What made you choose our system over the competitors'? ☐
   c) Who were the competitors? ☐
   d) Would you make the same decision again? ☐

9. What is the best way to persuade your manager to invest in your training?

a) Send an email and ask ❏

b) Tell your manager about the features of the training ❏

c) Make sure your training fits in the budget ❏

d) Sell your idea, explaining the benefits the company will get from your enhanced skill ❏

10. Which of the following statements is true?

a) Be sure you are well trained before going out on your first sales call ❏

b) Sales managers can't teach you anything ❏

c) Customers can't teach you anything ❏

d) You can learn from every sales call ❏

TUESDAY

Grasp the buying motives

A university professor I know shocks his class by saying, 'No one makes any decision in life that doesn't benefit himself in some way.'

The students always protest, 'Surely that's not true. People often do things for humanitarian reasons. There are church groups. There are people who do things unselfishly.'

'Yes,' the professor counters, 'that's true. But let's look under the surface. What motivates them? What makes them take their decision? What do *they* get out of it?'

Then he explains that carrying out even noble or humanitarian actions makes people feel good. This is the benefit to them.

Gradually, the students learn to examine the motives behind decisions and to look for what drives people. They discover that the benefits people gain can be psychological as well as material.

Think of this as it relates to your own sales situation. What benefits do your customers get? Don't think about what the product does. Think about the benefit to the buyer.

Today you will learn the best way to:

● find the customer's buying motives
● check your assumptions
● match benefits to needs and motives
● present your product or service.

Find the buying motives

Perhaps you've heard this saying: 'The person who asks the questions is in control of the meeting.'

In order to be in control of your success, it's necessary to ask questions, but not just any questions. They must be questions that lead you to the customer's needs and buying motives.

I remember once discussing a prospective client with a new employee. I told my employee that it would be his job at the upcoming meeting to ask questions that would lead us to the buying motive of the prospect. He said he could do it, because he considered himself to be a good conversationalist.

After 20 minutes with the customer, my employee was taking the conversation in all directions *except* to discover why he might want our service. I had to jump in and steer the conversation in the right direction – that of the prospect's needs and what benefits he might gain from our sales training courses. My employee hadn't learned to *target* his conversation in a certain direction. It was a hit-and-miss approach.

Hit and miss doesn't work in selling because we don't have the time we have in social relationships. We have to ask precise questions that lead us in the direction of the answers we need in order to identify our clients' needs, and then stress the corresponding benefits. Such questions could be:

- 'What would you be expecting from a supplier?'
- 'What benefit would you be hoping for?'
- 'What one thing could we offer to convince you to change suppliers and work with us?'

These three precise and directive questions lead you in the direction of finding out the needs and motives of your client. Now think of more questions. Create your own list.

Think of yourself as a sailor with the rudder of your sailing boat in the grip of your hand. As your boat goes slightly off course, you move the rudder to bring it back on course.

To become a powerful and directive questioner we need only think of ourselves as sailors. When the conversation starts to go off course, when it starts to wander aimlessly in this direction or that, we need to bring it back on course. For example, we could say, 'Yes, I see what you mean. That's important to know. I remember you said earlier that you wanted a high-clarity screen...' and so we are back on track. We could then continue with, 'What benefits would you be looking for – higher productivity, faster turnround, less frustration?'

TIP *Practise, practise and practise bringing the conversation back to ascertaining the customer's needs and motives.*

The person who asks the questions sets the direction. We must make sure we know what direction we want to go in.

Get the logical and emotional motives

We can actually help our buyer on two levels: the logical level and the emotional level.

Another way to look at this is to say that every corporate purchase has a benefit to the corporation and a benefit to the individual. Most salespeople focus only on the logical or corporate benefit. Yet the emotional or individual benefit can be, and often is, far more powerful and persuasive.

Why not go away to a quiet place and list your prospects. What are their emotional or individual buying motives?

● What do they need and want?
● What benefits can I match to their needs?

Check your assumptions

The title of this chapter is 'Grasp the buying motives'. Yet sales are lost because people assume they already *know* what the customer wants.

Using the following checklist to prompt you, list all the assumptions you can think of that you and your colleagues may be making about the needs and buying motives of your prospects. Examine them and ask why you have made each assumption. Is it something the customer said? Is it something ingrained from the last customer? Is it something a colleague has said about the customer? All of your assumptions need to be validated.

Checklist of assumptions about needs and buying motives

List the assumptions you and your colleagues may be making about the needs and buying motives of your prospects.

- Price (too high). Why?
- Price (too low). Why?
- Extras (important). Why?
- Extras (not important). Why?
- Distance
- Delivery time
- Features
- Benefits
- Service

The best way to check your assumptions is to call your customers and ask if your assumptions are right. Then you must *listen* to their answers and reshape your presentation or proposal accordingly. If it's a team sell, you will also need to convince your colleagues to avoid these costly assumptions.

Thus we realize how much time and effort we've lost barking up the wrong tree, and change our approach to selling. If you really want to excel in avoiding assumptions, track the reasons for every sale you lose or have lost. The best companies do just that.

In my book *Secrets of the World's Top Sales Performers*, I describe how the Sony sales team sit together and examine their approach and assumptions. They don't point fingers in order to place the blame outside; instead, they decide what caused the loss and how to overcome it next time.

During your analyses, you'll discover that making assumptions about buying motives is fatal. It's a fast cure and a lesson every professional needs to learn.

A common deadly assumption

When calling to find out why the business was lost, you'll discover that there were pressures within the organization that eluded you.

One of our seminar delegates told the story of working closely for several months with the managing director of a company to identify his needs. He thought everything was perfect until he presented the final proposal and discovered that the production director also had influence.

What did he do wrong? His error is common and painful. He assumed that the MD's authority was enough. He didn't identify the people who influenced the purchase decision and therefore didn't find out their needs.

Match benefits to needs and motives

One computer systems saleswoman in America is constantly ranked at the top of her national sales team. Janet achieves 190 per cent of her target year after year.

Let's look at the critical difference between Janet's approach, which keeps her at the top end, and the approach of salespeople whose performance is average.

She has an invaluable two-tier approach.

1 First she visits the prospective client on a fact-finding mission, and interviews them thoroughly to ascertain their needs and motives. She also makes sure she interviews everyone who influences the buying decision.
2 Only then does she present the benefit of her product and in such a way that it precisely meets the customer's needs.

She focuses all her energy and all her words on what the customer will gain from the system. Her preparation time goes into thinking about how the system can match the needs of each individual and therefore justify the costs in their minds.

The average salesperson doesn't hit the bull's eye because their questioning process fails them. Their needs analysis and motive analysis are missing or inadequate. They don't follow the seven vital rules and so do not sell as often as they could.

During your 'think' before your presentation, you will have made notes, listed those who influence the decision and thought about everyone's needs. You will have looked at the presentation from all sides, as if it were a three-dimensional picture. You'll have thought about all angles in preparation for your next approach to them.

You might want to put it all on a computer graph or on paper, as in the following example.

Our product benefits	A	B	C	D	etc.
Needs of Company X					
1.					
2.					
3.					
Needs of Company Y					
1.					
2.					
3.					
Emotional needs Customer A					
1.					
2.					
3.					
Emotional needs Customer B					
1.					
2.					
3.					

Seven vital rules for selling

1 Never assume you know the customer's needs and motives.

2 Identify all individuals who influence the purchase decision.

3 Interview to uncover needs and motives.

4 Discover the logical and psychological motives.

5 Go away and think.

6 Express the product or service benefits that match the customer's needs and motives.

7 Only then present to the customer with complete focus on their buying motives.

MONDAY

TUESDAY

WEDNESDAY

THURSDAY

FRIDAY

SATURDAY

Present the product or service

Armed with our list of buying motives and the benefits we can offer to meet the customer's needs, we have nothing to fear. Now we see clearly what to present. When we go to our customer, we will not be 'winging it'. We will not be improvising. We will be presenting our product or service in such a way that they can see the benefit and justify it. Their logical and emotional needs will be met.

It will all fall into place because you will have given the customer's buying motive the pre-eminent position. You will have stepped into the customer's shoes and seen the situation from their point of view. You will be on their side of the fence and they will feel it.

Summary

Today we focused on ways to grasp the buying motives of our prospect. Our time is valuable, and we shouldn't waste it presenting features and benefits of our product or service that don't relate to that particular prospect.

Instead, we must spend our time productively, matching the needs of our prospective client to what we can offer. To discover these all-important needs, we simply need to guide conversations in that direction by asking the right questions. When we have discovered all the needs of our prospect, our job in selling becomes easy and enjoyable. We skilfully link those needs to the benefits we offer, in order to have a successful sale!

Remember

The person who asks the questions guides the direction. Make sure you steer in the direction of the buying motives.

SUNDAY
MONDAY
TUESDAY
WEDNESDAY
THURSDAY
FRIDAY
SATURDAY

Fact-check (answers at the back)

1. What kind of questions lead to discovering the buying motives?
   a) General questions ❏
   b) Vague questions ❏
   c) Open-ended questions ❏
   d) Precise questions ❏

2. Which analogy best shows how to lead your discussion in the direction of your customer's needs and buying motives?
   a) You are a sailor; as your boat goes slightly off course, you move your rudder to bring it back on course. ❏
   b) You are a boxer fighting to win ❏
   c) You are a great conversationalist building rapport by talking ❏
   d) You are a bullfighter dodging left, right and centre ❏

3. What's true about buying motives?
   a) They are always logical, and never emotional ❏
   b) They are both logical and emotional ❏
   c) They are not important ❏
   d) They cause objections ❏

4. What do most ineffective salespeople only focus on?
   a) Logical or corporate benefit ❏
   b) Emotional benefit ❏
   c) Serious benefit ❏
   d) Elusive benefits ❏

5. What's likely to happen when you assume you know what the customer wants without asking?
   a) Customers are happy ❏
   b) Customers are angry ❏
   c) Sales are lost ❏
   d) You look good ❏

6. What is a common deadly assumption?
   a) The boss always makes the final decision ❏
   b) The Finance Director always makes the final decision ❏
   c) The department head makes the final decision ❏
   d) All of the above ❏

7. The average salesperson doesn't succeed because their question process fails them. Why?
   a) Their needs analysis is inadequate ❏
   b) Their motive analysis is missing ❏
   c) They make assumptions instead of asking questions ❏
   d) All of the above ❏

8. What should you do before making your final sales presentation?
   a) Make notes about needs and benefits ❏
   b) List those who influence the decision ❏
   c) Look at the presentation from all sides, as with a three-dimensional picture ❏
   d) All of the above ❏

9. What do you need to do in order to have nothing to fear in your presentation?
   a) Relax and improvise ❏
   b) Go armed with a list of buying motives and benefits you can offer that meet their needs ❏
   c) Give a slick presentation ❏
   d) Memorize everyone's name ❏

10. What will you feel after you have done a complete needs and benefits analysis?
a) Great about yourself ☐
b) As if you have stepped into the customer's shoes and seen the situation from their point of view ☐
c) Exhausted, but feeling good that it was worth the effort ☐
d) More committed to selling ☐

WEDNESDAY

Conquer objections: turn them to your advantage

The instructor at a seminar I attended early in my career was a world-class expert on the subject of self-motivation. 'Most people are clueless about obstacles,' he told us. 'They come to the first obstacle in the road between themselves and their goal, and they stop dead in their tracks.' He said that people are surprised to find obstacles in life, and yet obstacles are around us continually. 'When we learn to accept that obstacles are a normal part of life, we are on a winning track,' he said.

And so it is with selling. An objection is nothing more than a minor obstacle, and often it can be turned to our advantage.

When we handle objections, whether in selling or in everyday life, we're dealing with human factors, with people's need to be heard, and to be recognized for their opinions, fears, doubts and misunderstandings.

This takes finesse on our part. It takes time to stop and think. It takes determination to do things a new way.

Today you will learn about:

- clearing objections to improve your results
- using a foolproof objection-clearing technique
- mastering price objections
- closing despite objections.

Improve results by clearing objections

Let's look at two examples in which we can apply the objections process to improve our results. Some years ago I gave a speech to 150 people from a political party that had previously taken our sales and marketing course.

After my speech, I asked some of them, 'What have you implemented from the course so far?' Their immediate answer was, 'Better ways of handling the objections of our electorate.' Thus we see the importance of being able to sell and defend our ideas. The same is true in the workplace and in all areas of life.

Here is a second example, a true story told to me by one of our instructors about the power of the objection process in personal life. By using this process, he reported that he had improved his relationship with his teenage daughter tremendously. After applying the three-part objection technique in a conversation with her, she told him that it was the first time she felt he had really listened to her. Thus her attitude and co-operation improved enormously.

In selling, if we don't clear the objection, it lingers like smoke in the mind of our customers. We must clear it just as we clear smoke from a room. Think of a large fan blowing the smoke out through an open window. That's what you're doing with the objection-clearing process.

Use the objection-clearing technique

This foolproof three-part process can have extraordinary results for you too. The steps are:

1 the 'prelude cushion' (psychological)
2 the explanation (logical)
3 the clarification question (psychological).

The prelude cushion

Our 'prelude cushion' prepares people to listen by melting down their defences.

You may think it logical to focus on your explanation segment, but this will fall on deaf ears unless you break down the defences of the customer first. When I refer to the 'customer' in this case, of course I'm referring to our listener, be it our boss, our spouse, our child, our political constituents, our colleague or our client.

The prelude cushion is when we take time to sympathize with the customer, to line up on their side and see their point of view first, before we start on our logical explanation. If the customer says no, we must start again with our prelude segment. But the chances are that they won't, because our words have made them feel that we understand their concerns. We didn't ride roughshod over their objections.

The prelude cushion gives the other person a chance:

- to cool down
- to realize we're on their side
- to feel understood
- to have their concerns validated
- to save face
- to build a rapport with us.

Do you think those points are important to the person with the objection? Of course they are. That's why it improved our instructor's relationship with his daughter, in the example above. She felt as though her father had taken time to listen to her and care about her point of view.

What people want from us

We need to think about this point carefully. Isn't that what people want from us in any situation – to be listened to and to have their concerns recognized? And isn't that what's missing when we bypass the prelude segment and go straight to our explanation segment?

Don't make that mistake. If you do, you'll just be handling objections the old way and you'll have no improvement.

No matter how good your explanation segment, it won't sink in until you convince people that you sympathize with and value their concerns.

Master price objections

Let's look at a hot subject with salespeople – overcoming the price objection. First let's look at the difference between success and failure. The truth is that most ineffective salespeople *think* that they could sell *if* their price were lower.

However, most top salespeople don't consider price to be an obstacle. Why? Think about this because the chances are that you've fallen into the same trap from time to time.

Why do the top performers breeze past the price objections when others are blocked?

The reasons are *attitude* and *understanding*. If we think our price is too high, you can be sure we'll transmit that to our customer. If we think our price is too high, we won't look for the benefits that justify the price.

Would our companies stay in business if the price didn't justify the benefits? Probably not.

If the price really is too high, then it's time to cure the problem or change jobs. The point is this: *don't* make the mistake of the majority of ineffective salespeople, which is to try to ignore price justifications.

We must get out there and *learn* price justifications as the top performers do. That will form our logical explanation segment. And we must remember to prelude our price justification.

Why not put the technique into practice and see what you can achieve? I think you'll be surprised. You can work on your answers today by using the three-part objection-clearing process chart near the end of this chapter and the following case study.

The process in action

'I like your product, but the price is too high,' our customer says. At this point we don't know what he means by 'too high'. Is it higher than the competition for exactly the same thing, higher than his budget or higher than his expectation? But we can't ask yet because we haven't broken down the resistance.

1 The prelude cushion

Think about what your prelude should be. It must be right for you and your customer. Fill the appropriate response into the three-part process chart, perhaps something like this:

'Yes, I can understand your concern about price, Miss Whitehill. With the economy the way it is, businesses have to make every penny count. In fact, you're not alone. A lot of our clients told us they were worried about price before they used our service. Yet afterwards they come back and tell us they had a 100 per cent payback within six months.'

2 The explanation

Now we're making our transition to the logical explanation. In our prelude we sympathized with *the customer's* concern. We even said others felt the same. We're going out of our way to prove we understand the concern from the customer's point of view.

Now, what *are* our price justification benefits? What reasons do we have that will justify the expenditure? Chances are that you'll find dozens when you start digging.

You'll be most effective if you get these from current and past customers, because you'll have high credibility stories to tell your clients. For example, 'Mr Phillips at Tarmaco told me last week that they reduced their down time by 30 minutes per day with our service. This amounted to £10,000 per year.'

We should always match the customer's buying motives to the benefits we put forward. We won't talk about down time if it's irrelevant. We'll choose some benefit that does justify the price to that particular customer.

Brainstorm price justification

Look again at the three-part process chart below and list all the price justifications you can think of, then talk to colleagues and customers to expand the list. It might seem like a daunting task but, once you've done it, it will be a gold mine at your disposal.

Start your list now before you read on. Even if it's just one or two points scribbled on a scrap of paper, it will get you started. The first step is the hardest and we want to get you on the winning path. Remember, success is in our actions, as well as our realizations. We must be unrelenting with ourselves when we're forming new habits of success.

TIP *If you can't justify the price, your customer certainly can't, so your preparation today will win you great rewards tomorrow.*

3 The clarification question

Now it's time to nail down the closing with our clarification question: 'Have I satisfied your concerns on the price, Miss Whitehill?'

'Well, yes, but I'm still concerned about the set-up cost,' she responds.

Good. Now we know she's satisfied about the running costs, but she has a concern about the set-up costs. That's not a problem.

We use the three-part process again.

1 We start at the beginning, with another prelude cushion.
2 Then we go to the second step, the logical explanation. We give the benefits she'll receive in exchange for the price she pays for set-up.
3 Then we go to the third step, the clarification. Ask a question to see whether she accepts our explanation. Make a copy of the following chart for each of your prospects and fill it in as appropriate for them.

Three-part objection-clearing process chart

1 Prelude cushion	2 Explanation	3 Clarification question
(human/psychological factor)	(logical factor)	(human/psychological factor)
This opens the iron gate and breaks down the resistance.	This is the justification: benefits received in exchange for money paid out. **a** **b** **c** **d**	Does our customer understand and accept our explanation?

Close despite objections

We may never satisfy every concern a customer has. There will always be a competitor who offers something we don't offer. There will always be requests we can't fulfil. But when we can satisfy enough concerns to outweigh the doubts, we will succeed.

You can always use the direct approach: 'Margaret, we've discussed a checklist of ten requirements you hoped to meet. We are able to meet eight of these. They are the significant ones. I see those eight as being...' (We list the benefits and price justifications that relate to her.)

We ask, 'Does it sound like the kind of service you would benefit from?' *Thus you help the customer put the situation into perspective.* The chances are that eight out of ten of the requirements will be enough to meet their demands, especially if the requirements you can offer outweigh the ones you can't offer.

Be armed ahead

In preparation for your success ahead, you'll want to be armed with a list of likely objections and responses. Copy the following chart and add as many sheets as you need to be prepared for most eventualities.

Use the answers you have prepared on this chart during sales presentations, telephone calls with prospective customers and even in written communication.

Think now about all the areas in which you can use the three-part objection-clearing process. Set a target today for improving your success rate in breaking down the iron gate of resistance and overcoming objections.

Now think of ways to:

● practise it
● remember to do it.

Reference chart of possible objections

	Prelude statement	Explanation statement	Clarification question
1 Price			
2 Delivery time			
3 Lack of expertise			

4 Other likely objections
   a
   b
   c			

Summary

Today we studied ways of overcoming the objections of our prospective customers, and even ways to turn objections to our advantage.

We looked in depth at an effective three-part process for overcoming objections, be they on price, delivery time or any other factor.

We learned that if we don't cushion our response to an objection, it will fall on deaf ears. We learned that the explanation segment of our response must be one that *matches* our client's needs. We learned to end our three-part process for overcoming objections with a simple question: 'Does this satisfy your concern?' By doing so, we will assess whether the concern is gone, so that it won't linger like smoke, or whether we need to readdress the concern and bring it to a positive conclusion.

When you master the three-part process, nothing will hold you back! You'll go from strength to strength in your career. So start now and make this your speciality.

Remember

The prelude cushion is the key to having your explanation accepted and the objection overcome.

Fact-check (answers at the back)

1. Learning to overcome objections is a useful tool to use with whom?
   a) Teenagers ❑
   b) Politicians ❑
   c) Customers ❑
   d) Everyone ❑

2. In selling, what will happen if we don't clear an objection?
   a) It will go unnoticed ❑
   b) No one cares ❑
   c) It lingers like smoke in the mind of our customers ❑
   d) It's good for business ❑

3. In handling objections, what must we do before we put the spotlight on the explanation?
   a) Break down the defences and fears of the customer ❑
   b) Change the subject ❑
   c) Make sure the customer understands the features of the product or service ❑
   d) Make sure the customer understands the benefits of the product or service ❑

4. In the three-part process of handling objections, what does the prelude segment do?
   a) It gives the customer a chance to feel understood ❑
   b) It allows the customer's concerns to be validated ❑
   c) It lets the customer build rapport with us ❑
   d) All of the above ❑

5. What does every customer – and every person we know – want?
   a) To be listened to ❑
   b) To have their concerns recognized ❑
   c) For us to value their concerns ❑
   d) All of the above ❑

6. What's the best way to handle price objection?
   a) Learn price justification ❑
   b) Remember to prelude our price justification ❑
   c) Put the three-part process into practice. ❑
   d) All of the above ❑

7. What is the explanation segment?
   a) The logical explanation ❑
   b) The emotional explanation ❑
   c) The contrary segment ❑
   d) All of the above ❑

8. What's the most important question for you to ask when ending the objection process?
   a) 'Shall we move on?' ❑
   b) 'Have I answered your concerns about that?' ❑
   c) 'When would you like to start?' ❑
   d) 'Did I explain that well?' ❑

9. What should we do when we can't satisfy every concern a customer has?
a) We should withdraw ❏
b) We can close anyway if the benefits outweigh the objections ❏
c) We should talk the customer out of his or her concern ❏
d) We should refer them to our competitor ❏

10. What is the purpose of preparing a chart with likely objections and responses?
a) For sales presentations ❏
b) For telephone calls to prospective customers ❏
c) For written communication ❏
d) For all of the above ❏

THURSDAY

Master successful presentations and closings

There is nothing magic about closing a sale. If all the component parts are there, you need only ask a question such as, 'Does this seem right for you?' or 'When would you like to begin?' *Then* the business will be more likely to fall into your lap. But what are those all-important component parts?

There are eight component parts to successful sales presentations and closings. Seven of these lead up to asking for the business while building commitment along the way. Your job is to become an expert in each of the eight segments.

You have been practising all the skills involved throughout your life. It's simply a matter of putting them together in the right order – in a 'presentation train'.

Today you will build your expertise by learning about the eight parts of the presentation train, which are:

- finding out the corporate buying motive
- finding out the personal buying motive
- showing your product expertise
- understanding competitors' strengths and weaknesses
- linking needs to benefits
- overcoming objections
- reviewing needs and benefits
- the successful close.

The presentation train

Most of the segments of the presentation train involve asking questions, sincerely and with genuine interest. Some involve presenting facts about your product or service that link to your customer's needs.

The engine comes first. In successful selling, determining the buying motive drives the content of the presentation. And last comes the caboose, the final car on the train. In selling, that's where you close your sales. And in the middle will be six wagons, representing the other factors leading to your close.

1 ASK – Find out the customer's corporate buying motive.
2 ASK – Find out the customer's personal buying motive.
3 KNOW – Show your product expertise.
4 KNOW – Understand the competition's strengths and weaknesses.
5 TELL – Make links between needs and benefits.
6 TELL – Overcome objections.
7 REVIEW – Refocus on needs and benefits.
8 ASK – Their decision needs your closing question.

Imagine each part of your presentation process as a separate wagon on a freight train. Each wagon is splendidly painted and filled with jewels.

Imagine that we are the railway inspectors. We walk along the side of the wagons together, sliding open the doors, and we see that each is filled with precious blue, yellow and green jewels. These jewels represent:

● facts
● answers
● links.

The blue jewels represent the facts. The yellow jewels represent the answers we get. The green jewels represent the links between them.

In your sales presentation, when you combine the facts with the answers to your questions, you'll be able to make critical links. These links will be the green light to your sale.

1 Ask about the corporate buying motive

Let's have a look inside the engine, which is reserved for the customer's corporate buying motive. It will be almost empty when we first slide the door open. There will be a few facts here about why *most* people buy your product or service, but no specific facts about why *this* customer wants your product.

Assumptions don't count in sales. But as we ask questions, our engine will fill with more and more facts, more and more jewels to help us link the buying motive to the benefits we have to offer.

The difference between you, a top sales performer, and a mediocre sales performer is that you will ask and ask and ask until your engine is *filled* with facts and answers. You'll find out the buying motives of every decision maker and every decision influencer. Each answer, each fact, will add another authentic, precious jewel to your engine.

The mediocre sales performers will not take time to ask because they assume that this customer is like all the others. Their false assumptions will lead them to impure links. The benefits they offer to the client will therefore be right for other customers but not necessarily right for this customer. Their time will be spent in vain.

We won't let this happen to us because we realize that the time spent here is the most valuable of all.

2 Ask about the personal buying motive

Most ineffective salespeople don't even push open the door to this first wagon to look inside for the personal buying motive. They assume that the engine, the corporate buying motive, is all-important. Yes, of course, we can't sell without satisfying ourselves that the engine is full of valuable jewels, but we must not discount another, vitally important factor: how will we get our prospect to push for consensus within his or her organization to buy from us?

If our prospect is not personally motivated, why should he or she bother? After all, they have a job to do. Our sales efforts are an intrusion in their busy schedule.

We must identify *what's in it for them*. What is it that can motivate them personally? Is it:

● saving time
● improving prestige
● reducing chaos
● reducing stress
● improving morale
● being up to date
● career advancement
● more free time?

We have to *ask*. We have to fill our wagon with genuine jewels of answers and facts in order to create the genuine links necessary to sell.

3 Know and show product expertise

As we're turning their situation around and around in our minds, the links are building up faster and faster. We have our product expertise: those blue jewels in our second wagon are the facts about our product and service. Now we are pouring in the yellow jewels – the answers to all our questions about the customer's corporate and personal buying motives.

The yellow and blue jewels are merging together in our mind, and green sparks are radiating from them. Those are our links – the combination of needs and benefits which are the reasons people will buy.

Naturally, *your* wagon is brimming with knowledge. You've painstakingly talked to current customers to find out why they use your products. You've found out what benefits they get. You've built up first-hand stories about these benefits. You *know* what you have to offer to prospective customers in every detail. You've consulted your literature and your internal experts. You *know*.

4 Know the competition's strengths and weaknesses

Don't be afraid when you look inside this third wagon.

Knowledge is power: the more we know, the better the position we will be in to defend the benefits we can offer.

Our competitor may have some excellent features but, if those features are not important to our client, we can still sell our benefits and win. The important thing is to be informed about what the competition *does* offer. Then we won't be taken by surprise. We'll have time to turn it around in our mind, to become comfortable with it in a matter-of-fact way, to accept it as a feature but put it in perspective.

'Yes,' we can say to ourselves, 'they have this feature; we have that. Now let's see who needs what. Let's look at the combination of benefits. Let's look at the cost of their benefits and of our benefits, and find out who is willing to pay what for those benefits.'

Then, when a customer says that our competitor has feature A, we'll be able to say, 'Yes, how do you feel about that feature? There are many features in the marketplace today. We've created ours by researching what our users most wanted for the price, ease of use,' etc. We then help the customer put it into perspective.

Key questions

- Do they really need what the competitors offer?
- Is it really an advantage?
- Will they really use it or is there a downside?
- What will it cost the customer either financially or in terms of learning, time or energy?
- What will they have to give up in order to gain that?
- What are the start-up and continuation costs?
- What does your package of features and benefits have to offer over theirs?

By helping them to re-evaluate it, they may see that it's not important at all. The last salesperson may have made them feel they couldn't live without this 'all-singing, all-dancing' feature. But you, through your thoroughness in asking about their buying motives, can help them reflect.

Because knowledge is power, and our wagon is full of knowledge about the competitors, we're in a position of strength, not weakness. We have little to fear. We'll be able to make links that work for us *and* for the client.

5 Tell them how their needs link to your benefits

This is the moment of truth. I mean that literally. If we have the truth in terms of the buyer's needs and motives, if we have all the true facts about what our products can do, then we'll be able to make these links which give the buyer the mental green light to buy.

Selling today is not a manipulative process. Selling is helping the customer *see* what we have to offer and how it meets *their* needs. Notice that there are two parts to this and that the second part is the key to success:

1 what we have to offer
2 how it meets their needs.

Many ineffective salespeople focus on only the first part. They don't stop to realize that a customer wouldn't want to buy from someone who says, 'We can do this, we can do this, we can do this.'

Who is the most important person in the world? The customer is, of course. A salesperson who talks only about their product and what it can do will not make the customer feel important or cared about. It's the *link to their needs* that makes the sale.

We can't make this link without asking the customer what they want, what benefit they see, what their objective is, how they will use it. We don't do it as an interrogation, but rather from a position of consultative concern, of really trying to help. Don't make the mistake of the ineffective salesperson, doing only half the job. You'll get only half the results. Do the whole job – make the link. Tell them how it meets their needs. Do this and your sales will more than double. This is true in every industry, from retail to aerospace, from products and services to politics and education.

Stating the link between benefits and needs

Customer X

Need: Customer wants to reduce their department's annual overheads by £15,000.

Benefit: Say, 'Our system saves 20 per cent man hours over your current system.'

Link: Say, 'You'll be able to do without your two temporary members of staff, saving £30,000. This £30,000 in overhead reduction will pay for the system in the first year and reduce your running costs by £15,000, which was your goal. From then on, you continue to save every year.'

Make a table like the one below to fill in the needs and benefits and the links between them for your own customers.

	Customer A	Customer B	Customer C
Need			
Benefit			
Link			

Once you have developed your link-building expertise, you'll be able to communicate it verbally or in writing or both, thus increasing your closing rate.

6 Tell them how objections can be overcome

Remember that objections can linger like smoke unless you address them. *You* won't let objections linger because you'll use the three-part objection technique you learned on Wednesday. You'll make your customer realize that you *do* sympathize, you *do* understand. Then you'll give the explanation, and then you'll check to see if their concern is satisfied.

Ineffective salespeople don't see this fifth wagon as full of helpful jewels. They see it as full of serpents and demons. They want to keep it locked shut. They want to skirt around it, staying as far away from it as possible *at all times*.

They want to sweep any hint of objection under the rug, hoping naïvely that it will never resurface. Little do they know that it smoulders there while the customer's mind becomes locked into the idea that their objection is reality. The customer is mentally packing their briefcase to go home while the ineffective salesperson continues to talk – *unheard*.

Your wagon, on the other hand, is filled with blue and yellow jewels, because you've studied the likely objections and solutions, and you've asked questions to find out what the concerns are.

You have the facts and answers. You therefore counter the objections quickly and easily, as if holding the hand of the customer and walking them through a maze.

7 Review the needs and benefits

This is the most rewarding stage because it reveals the big picture. It puts everything into perspective for the customer. We've discussed features, benefits, needs, motives and objections. Now we're ready for the big picture.

'You told me you wanted to achieve X, Y, and Z. Is this still the case?' we must ask. We're helping them refocus on their needs, cut out the extraneous and forget the glorified benefits offered by the competitors.

Next, we say, 'We've looked at our ability to meet X, Y and Z through these methods...' and put our benefits succinctly. We don't elaborate for so long that the customer forgets what X, Y and Z are.

Instead, we keep our choice of words focused on what they get, not what we give. 'With this machine, you can get your documents to your office in Australia in six seconds. This will help you meet your objective of speeding up your communication time in order to win contracts.'

We won't say, 'This machine gives you group 3, high-speed, digital transmission technology.' That's about the machine, not the customer. In addition, it doesn't mention his objective at all!

Yet that's how most uninitiated salespeople would handle their presentation. You won't, of course, because your wagon is filled with the links – the jewels you've created by combining the needs with your benefits. You've sifted through the important versus the unimportant benefits to the customer, and you stress the important ones.

Focus on the benefits the customer gets from your product or service rather than on what you are offering.

8 Ask for their decision

The last wagon, the caboose, is the most vital one of all.

Recent research has shown that four out of five buyers *expect* to be asked to buy and *wait* to be asked. They don't volunteer to buy because they expect us, as part of the selling process, to ask. They wait and, if it doesn't happen, the buying moment passes by.

Let's look at what causes the critical moment to pass. Several things could happen. A competitor could ask for the order and get it, or the customer could lose interest or divert their funds to another project.

The ineffective salesperson – who doesn't ask – loses. But your approach is different. From the beginning you have been thorough. You've been letting the customer know how your product or service can help them, thus building commitment each step of the way. Your approach has let them see themselves using and benefiting from the product.

Now when you ask for their decision, it's almost a foregone conclusion. The benefits are clear and they *line up exactly* with the customer's expressed needs.

You've been a catalyst in their search for the answer. You've helped them make their way through the maze of the unknown. You've helped them see the answer.

Now when you ask for their decision, it's not an abrupt surprise. It's not a pressured, stressful event, but a natural evolution. Our customer now expects a closing question, which will vary according to the situation.

Closing questions

- 'Will you be taking this, then?' we might ask at the retail counter.

- 'Does this seem like the kind of service which would benefit you?' we might ask in the sale of services.

- 'Are the advantages we offer more meaningful than the other suppliers'?' we might ask in system sales.

- 'Will you be working with us, then?'

- 'What implementation dates should we establish?'

Stop now and make a list of closing questions that feel right for you. Then when you get to this stage of your presentation, you won't have fear. Instead, you'll see your final wagon filled with jewels of preparation. You'll have question after question which you designed and which work for you and not someone else.

Look at the freight train diagram at the beginning of this chapter again. Do you know the secret of success over others who fail?

Build your expertise

Most ineffective salespeople have no freight train at all. They have only a little product knowledge. They ask no questions to ascertain needs – they assume they know. They make no links to needs. They talk about the product only instead of the benefits. They avoid objections whenever possible. And they don't ask for the business.

Would you want to hire a person like that to work for your business? Probably not, and yet many managers find they have no choice. They hire people, find ways to train them and motivate them and then hope for results.

The case is different with you. You're building your own professionalism, which makes you a rare commodity, like a needle in a haystack.

Keep up the good work. The rewards will be coming your way. By continuing to build your expertise in sales, you will be increasing your value to yourself and your company. Many men and women in sales, like myself, start their own companies, or are promoted to executive or CEO positions. They are elected to chair important community groups.

Why? Because they have learned to motivate, to look for people's needs, to communicate and meet those needs. Imagine that you are a CEO needing to convince your Board of something important. Now look at the freight train at the beginning of this chapter. Isn't your job of selling your idea to the Board the same as selling a product to your customer? Your expertise in sales will help you define *their* needs and motives, present the benefits of *your* idea and link it to their needs.

Summary

Today we discovered the eight parts of mastering successful sales presentations and closings. Each part is indispensable, and each part is linked to the part before and after it, rather like wagons in a freight train.

First, we saw the importance of fleshing out the corporate buying motive, and second the customer's personal buying motive. We discovered that the latter is often overlooked and leads to lost sales. Third, we looked at product expertise, and fourth at competitors' strengths and weaknesses. We saw that it's often easy to overcome our competitors' strengths, if we ask thorough questions about corporate buying motives and personal buying motives. In this way, we can build up our product's strengths as they relate to our customer's needs.

In the fifth and sixth parts, we linked needs to benefits and overcame objections. That left the road clear for our seventh part – the review of needs and benefits – and finally, our eighth part – the successful close.

Remember

Four out of five customers wait for us to ask for the order. Be sure to ask closing questions.

SUNDAY

MONDAY

TUESDAY

WEDNESDAY

THURSDAY

FRIDAY

SATURDAY

Fact-check (answers at the back)

1. What's dangerous about making assumptions about buying motives?
   a) You will most likely get it wrong ❏
   b) Assumptions lead to why most people buy, but not why this customer wants to buy ❏
   c) You waste a lot of time and most likely lose the sale ❏
   d) All of the above ❏

2. Why do mediocre sales performers not take time to ask about buying motives?
   a) They assume that this customer is like all the others ❏
   b) They use the shotgun approach and want to get out of the appointment as soon as possible ❏
   c) They haven't taken the time to learn how to ask questions ❏
   d) All of the above ❏

3. Customers have corporate and personal motives for buying. Name some personal motives.
   a) Saving time ❏
   b) Career advancement ❏
   c) Reducing stress ❏
   d) All of the above ❏

4. How do we discover buying motive?
   a) By asking ❏
   b) By telling ❏
   c) Through interrogation ❏
   d) Through espionage ❏

5. In selling, which is most important?
   a) What we have to offer ❏
   b) How our offer meets the customer's needs ❏
   c) How our offer saves the customer money ❏
   d) How our offer helps the customer's career ❏

6. Objections linger like what, if not answered?
   a) Smoke ❏
   b) Serpents ❏
   c) Iron gates of resistance ❏
   d) All of the above ❏

7. Why is the review of the customer's needs and benefits one of the most rewarding parts of the sales process?
   a) It reveals the big picture ❏
   b) It puts everything into perspective for the customer ❏
   c) It sets the scene for the close ❏
   d) All of the above ❏

8. In the sales process, what should we focus our words on?
   a) What we can offer ❏
   b) What benefits the customer can get ❏
   c) The features ❏
   d) Price savings ❏

9. What is the most important aspect of closing a sale?
   a) Showing strong interest ❏
   b) Asking for their decision ❏
   c) Making promises ❏
   d Loving your job ❏

76

10. What characterizes expert salespeople?
a) They are easy to train ❏
b) They are good talkers ❏
c) They are a rare commodity, like a needle in a haystack ❏
d) They are a dime a dozen ❏

FRIDAY

Create action-provoking systems

Most of you who are reading this book are high achievers by nature. You are open to new ways of achieving even higher results, especially if the efforts or changes involved will be minimal and the results will be exceptional.

And so it is with the tips in this chapter. When improving your tennis game, for example, a ten per cent change can bring you 100 per cent better results, and the same is true in selling.

Today we look at why 'action-provoking systems' are so important, the best ways to use them and their critical advantages over other systems.

As you read ahead, don't be misled by the word 'system'. It might be a word that alienates some of you. It might even send a chill through you. After all, salespeople are sometimes thought of as spontaneous and freewheeling – traits that often lead to their success.

However, when we refer to 'action-provoking systems' here, we're referring to ways you can:

- keep *yourself* on track
- save yourself time
- harness your effort and send it in the right direction.

Strike while the iron is hot

Striking while the iron is hot is a critical issue. If we follow up a direct mail letter or email by telephone two weeks after it's sent, our call will be one-fifth as effective as it would be if we called within the first two days.

This is because people forget 60 per cent of what they hear and read after two days. If we call shortly after the letter or email is sent, it will be fresh in their minds. If we call after three weeks, it won't.

The same is true of following up your prospect for a decision. What's the point of following up too late – after our competitor goes in or after our customer's budget is diverted?

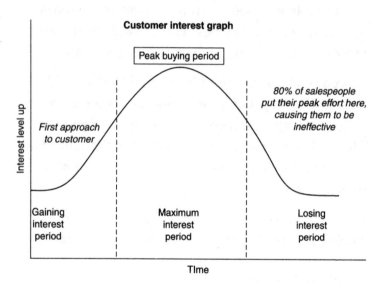

Customer interest graph

Peak buying period

First approach to customer

80% of salespeople put their peak effort here, causing them to be ineffective

Interest level up

Gaining interest period

Maximum interest period

Losing interest period

Time

Work hard or work sharp?

The majority of salespeople put their time and effort into the sales process too late. Because they don't have action-provoking systems, they do things when they have time rather than at the right time. Often this is too late.

An action-provoking system will help you use your time where it counts:

- closing the sales you have already started
- starting the correct number of new prospects necessary to meet your targets.

What's your experience?

What kind of system do you have now?

Perhaps your experience is something like John's, an experienced salesman who came to our course. He was looking desperately for a way to increase his sales, but didn't know which way to turn.

We asked him what sort of action-provoking system he had, and he said he wrote everything in his diary. He said he carried everything over to the new page. Yet he admitted it was a lot of work to carry it forward and easy to miss or forget some.

We looked at John's system and then showed him the matrix below. It can be created by hand or on the computer.

<table>
<tr><td colspan="9" align="center">Action-provoking system</td></tr>
<tr><td>June</td><td>1</td><td>2</td><td>3</td><td>4</td><td>5</td><td>6</td><td>7</td><td></td></tr>
<tr><td>1. Smith & Co</td><td>X</td><td></td><td></td><td></td><td></td><td></td><td></td><td></td></tr>
<tr><td>2. J Bloggs</td><td></td><td></td><td></td><td></td><td></td><td></td><td></td><td></td></tr>
<tr><td>3. Estman</td><td></td><td>X</td><td></td><td></td><td></td><td></td><td></td><td></td></tr>
<tr><td>4. Winters</td><td></td><td>X</td><td></td><td></td><td></td><td></td><td></td><td></td></tr>
<tr><td>5. Peak and Co</td><td></td><td></td><td></td><td></td><td></td><td></td><td></td><td></td></tr>
<tr><td>6. Johnston</td><td></td><td></td><td></td><td></td><td></td><td></td><td></td><td></td></tr>
<tr><td>7. Withers</td><td></td><td></td><td></td><td></td><td></td><td></td><td></td><td></td></tr>
<tr><td>8. Goodall & Co.</td><td></td><td>X</td><td></td><td></td><td></td><td></td><td></td><td></td></tr>
<tr><td>9. Jones Bros</td><td></td><td></td><td></td><td></td><td></td><td></td><td></td><td></td></tr>
<tr><td>10. Kent Air</td><td></td><td></td><td></td><td></td><td></td><td></td><td></td><td></td></tr>
<tr><td>11. P.V. Anchor</td><td>X</td><td></td><td></td><td></td><td></td><td></td><td></td><td></td></tr>
<tr><td>12. Bassett</td><td></td><td>X</td><td></td><td></td><td></td><td></td><td></td><td></td></tr>
</table>

'The beauty of this system,' we told him, 'is that we can walk into our office in the morning and see at a glance all our prime prospects. We know immediately which ones need action.

'On 1 June two companies need action from us. On 2 June four companies need action. They are the ones on lines 3, 4, 8 and 12. We just pull up those files and see what action is necessary.'

Advantages of an action-provoking system

This action-provoking system gives us two critical advantages.

1 We're not likely to forget anyone. Their name is already entered.
2 We see at a glance much more about our prospect.

Let's say we call someone five days in a row and we miss them each time. We'll mark an X on the next consecutive day to remind us to call.

Later we'll have more critical information. We'll be able to glance at our sheet and see the number of X marks. If we see five X marks side by side, we'll know our efforts aren't succeeding. If this is a hot prospect, we'd better redouble our efforts or take other action.

John looked sceptical, but he went away and tried it. He called us a month later and said that the results of his new system put him up 40 per cent on his sales figures after only 30 days.

The weakness of diary systems

'The diary system used to let me lose prospects too conveniently,' he told us. 'I've closed three sales this month by entering them into the matrix system. I know I would have turned the page and forgotten them in my old diary system, but because they were on the matrix I couldn't forget. It also made me more aware of my hard work on each prospect to date by seeing all my actions on one sheet. It made me more determined. I felt more in control.'

You may have the same reluctance that John had at first. You probably have a system that works for you. Fine. But ask yourself the following questions.

● How well is it working?
● How much is slipping through the net that I'm not aware of?

If you're looking for sales excellence, you have to turn over every stone of your present practices and see if there is a way of doing anything differently. You might find a way to make a small change in your practices that can get you considerably higher results.

Take today to examine your system and find its weak points. Then develop a new, improved system.

The weakness of computerized systems

'We have a perfect computerized system,' one salesman said. 'It tells us everything we've done for a prospect and what stage it's at.'

'Great,' we said. 'Does it tell you what day you have to take the next action? Does it show you on any given day a list of every prospect that needs action that day?'

'Well, I'm not sure,' he said. 'But we can pull up any prospect name and see the history of our actions.'

Think about what he's just said and see if you can find two fallacies. There's nothing wrong with history, but history is history. It doesn't provoke us to action on a certain day.

So there we have the first fallacy – confusing 'action taken' with action 'to be taken'.

Think again about the computer system of the salesman above and where you can see the second fallacy. When we asked him if he got a list of prospects that need action every day, he said he *wasn't sure*. What does that tell us about his use of the system? It tells us that he wasn't using it, at least not to help him prompt his daily actions.

There's no point in having systems we don't use, and it becomes even more dangerous to think we have systems that help us when in fact they don't.

Record systems for prospecting

What we're looking for is an action-*provoking* system, not historical record keeping. We want a report that lets us see two things at a glance:

● a list of critical actions at the beginning of each day
● every prospect that should *have been* actioned in the past, with the number of days outstanding next to it (like an aged debtors' report which accountants use).

Only then do we have a good system. Only then do we know if we are striking while the 'iron is hot'.

Here's a useful manual system if you have hundreds of prospects to deal with at once. This system consists of two files. It's especially useful for telesales and telephone appointments.

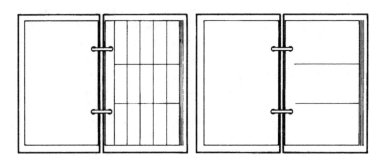

Action-provoking
ring binder 1

Prospect information
ring binder 2

In file 1 we have 52 sheets or printouts, each representing one week of the year. On each sheet there is a week number, date, and days of the week across the top.

Down the side there is a place to list:

- new prospects
- follow-up prospects
- appointment confirmations.

Each sheet looks like the one shown here.

Action-provoking file 1				
Week number .... Date				
New prospects				
Mon	Tues	Wed	Thurs	Fri
O				
Follow-up prospects				
O				
Appointment confirmations				

On Monday, we walk into the office knowing that *we must activate a certain number of new prospects*. This number depends on our yearly target, which we've broken down to a daily figure. Our prospects might come from a phone book or a Chamber of Commerce list, an industry list or a list of direct mail letters or emails already sent.

Now we are ready to follow each up by telephone. We go to our second file, which holds our prospect information.

Each sheet looks like this:

Prospect information file 2

Company name   Code number   A 103
Person
Title
Address
Tel number
Contact date and discussion details

O

Company name   Code number   A 104
Person
Title
Address
Tel number
Contact date and discussion details

O

Company name   Code number   A 105
Person
Title
Address
Tel number
Contact date and discussion details

Three or more prospects can fit easily on one page. Because of the volume of prospects, we give each a code number, which is easier to fit on to one sheet in the action-provoking ring binder.

By Monday night our sheet will look like this:

You'll see that most prospects have been spoken to. These

Action-provoking file 1				
Week number			Date	
New prospects				
Mon *A 105*	Tues *A105*	Wed	Thurs	Fri
~~A 106~~				
~~A 107~~				
○ ~~A 108~~				
A 109	*A 109*			
~~A 110~~				
Follow-up prospects				
~~A 63~~				
~~A 22~~				
○ ~~A 37~~				
A 88	*A 88*			
~~A 94~~				
Appointment confirmations				
A 80	*A 80*			
~~A 26~~				
~~A 37~~				

have diagonal lines through them. Prospects A105, 109, 88 and 80 have not been reached and therefore they are listed for action on Tuesday.

All records can be kept in the prospect information file, or on a laptop for easy portability.

When we get enough detail on one prospect, we may choose to open a separate file for them, on our computer or in the filing cabinet.

Take time to think of what system will work for you. Ask yourself the following questions.

- Where will I be when I use the system: in the car, at my desk, etc?
- How many entries will I need per day, per week and per month?
- What size book or record sheets do I need?
- Where will I store back-up information?
- What should the system look like?
- Who else will use it?
- Who will enter the prospect names?
- Who will enter the next actions required and the dates by which they must be done?
- What time of day will I take the actions, e.g. phone calls for appointments, phone calls for follow-up?

Add other questions to suit your situation.

Without an action-provoking system, we don't have the support system we need. Our energy is fragmented and at the end of the month we're disappointed we didn't get the results we hoped for.

Take today to design an action-provoking system to make your efforts effective.

Summary

Today we saw the importance of having a self-created, action-provoking system. Created by you, just for you, it will be easy to use, and portable if necessary. Perhaps it will be computerized, perhaps not.

Your system's most significant feature is that it will cue you to *what you need to do* each and every day. If it records only *what has been done*, it is not an action-provoking system but merely a data collection system. It will not help you take the actions today needed to reach your target. It won't help you double your income or gain a promotion or start your own business. While it may be useful for data collection, it will be largely a waste of time with regard to reaching your targets.

An action-provoking system, however, will take you above and beyond the league of 80 per cent of salespeople – the ineffective ones who put their effort in too late. Your system will keep you on track, striking while the iron is hot and closing while the customer still has interest...*not* pushing water up hill with a rake, after their interest is lost!

Remember
Your action-provoking system puts you in control.

Fact-check (answers at the back)

1. What percentage of salespeople put most of their effort into closing a sale after it's too late?
   a) 40% ❏
   b) 80% ❏
   c) 20% ❏
   d) 10% ❏

2. What's the most important period of the buying cycle?
   a) Gaining interest period ❏
   b) Maximum interest period ❏
   c) Losing interest period ❏
   d) All of the above ❏

3. What's the main reason so many salespeople put effort in too late and miss the sale?
   a) They don't have action-provoking systems ❏
   b) They do things when they have time ❏
   c) They don't want to be seen as being too aggressive ❏
   d) All of the above ❏

4. What are the benefits to you of having an action-provoking system?
   a) It will help you use your time where it counts ❏
   b) It will help you close the sales you have already started ❏
   c) It will help you start the correct number of new prospects necessary to meet your targets ❏
   d) All of the above ❏

5. What systems are least likely to help you reach your targets?
   a) A diary system ❏
   b) Ones that don't list every prospect ❏
   c) Systems that record what has been done, rather than what needs to be done ❏
   d) All of the above ❏

6. What must computerized systems do to work well and help you reach your goals?
   a) Tell you everything you've done for a prospect, and what stage the sales is at ❏
   b) Tell you what day you have to take the next action ❏
   c) Show you, on any given day, a list of every prospect that needs action that day ❏
   d) All of the above ❏

7. What's the biggest failure of sales systems?
   a) Confusing action taken with actions to be taken ❏
   b) Messy documents ❏
   c) Hard-to-carry systems ❏
   d) Too much data ❏

8. What specific information does a sales system need to help you reach your goals the fastest?
   a) Data about history about the prospect ❏
   b) A new list of prospects ❏
   c) Advice codes for each prospect ❏
   d) A list of prospects that need action every day ❏

9. When creating action-provoking systems, which questions are useful to ask yourself?

a) Where will I be when I use the system: in the car, at my desk, etc.? ❏
b) Who else will use it? ❏
c) Who will enter the next actions required and the dates by when they must be done? ❏
d) All of the above ❏

10. What will happen if you don't have an action-provoking system?

a) You won't have the support system you need ❏
b) Your energy will be fragmented ❏
c) You'll be disappointed you didn't get the results you hoped for ❏
d) All of the above ❏

SATURDAY

Implement motivation and support systems

People often tell me that they find the hardest part of selling is keeping themselves motivated and on track. In the sales profession, we don't often have the support network we had in other jobs. We usually have no one setting our deadlines or telling us what projects to work on next.

One woman I know was an Olympic swimmer, with all the skills of a self-disciplined person when it came to goal setting and practice. When she started her own company selling from home, she told me, 'Christine, I don't have a structure any more, like I had in my old job.'

What she didn't realize was that she had to create her own structure and support systems. The good news is that, after applying the principles of this book, she was up and running, drawing on the motivation she had had as an Olympic athlete.

And so it will be with you. Today you will learn how to:

- be your own cheerleader
- devise your own support systems
- stay positive when the going gets tough
- eliminate the doldrums and self-criticism
- dare to be different
- overcome roadblocks and move quickly to your goal.

Be your own cheerleader

'Everyone gets into the doldrums,' my first sales manager told our sales team, 'but it's up to each of you to get yourselves out of them.'

It would be nice if we all had sales managers who could coach us and encourage us at every turn, like the best football coach. But that's not practical. Managers are occupied with many activities, and they can't possibly know our personality and motivational needs as well as we can. Most importantly, though, think who our success is reliant on: them or us?

Since we can't wait for someone else to motivate us and set up our motivation systems for us, we have to do it ourselves. In effect we have to carry our own cheerleader or football coach in our mind.

What motivation and support systems can you put into place which will allow you to reach the top?

What support do I need?

Think about your own situation carefully. What kind of support and encouragement do you want when you have a 'down' day? What kind of support do you want on normal days?

Be specific and complete your own list. It might include support for:

- goal setting
- reaching a particular milestone
- doing a mundane task consistently
- cold calling
- getting appointments
- boosting morale
- confidence building.

Today we'll study the motivation and support systems of the top achievers so that you can choose those that would work for you and put them into place immediately. They include:

- people who can support you
- developing a positive attitude
- acknowledging your strengths
- doing things differently
- overcoming obstacles
- defining your goals.

Create personal support

What do you need from people? One top salesman talks to his wife from his mobile phone four times a day. He likes having someone to share his progress with, his ups and downs, his trials and tribulations.

Decide what support you want from people. All of us have people in our lives willing to support us, especially if we're willing to support them in our turn.

Who do you have? Open your mind to an expanded group of potential supporters. They might be partners, friends, co-workers, sales or other managers, people from your social groups, progressive thinkers, the community, Chambers of Commerce, new acquaintances or customers.

Be specific about the kind of support you want, referring to the list in the box above. Then set your goals, and share your progress with your supporter. Just reporting your progress to someone every day for a week, for example, can start you on a new path or help you form a new habit. I do this with a friend of mine who also owns her own company.

Think now. Who can you talk to? You'll be surprised at how many people there are who would like to have this support reciprocated.

Stay positive

What are the chances that your customer will be positive if you aren't? The answer is zero.

We all have negative thoughts that pass through our minds, but it's our choice whether to hang on to them or not. The first step is to notice what our thoughts are.

Notice your thoughts

If you were to count the number of thoughts that flash through the mind in one minute, you would reach well over 60. We can't hold on to every one, so why not pick the positive ones? So often in life we give in to the negative ones, forgetting that we are in charge of either holding on to or releasing those thoughts.

Release the negative

One top sales executive I interviewed for my book, *Secrets of the World's Top Sales Performers*, has developed his own mind-clearing process, which is very effective.

He takes a walk after work to review how the day has gone, deciding what mistakes he's made, what to do about them and what to do differently next time. Then he releases any negative thoughts or guilt remaining about his mistakes.

In other words, he concentrates on correcting his mistakes rather than downgrading himself for making them in the first place.

Think now about what system you can put into place to:

● listen to your thoughts
● concentrate on correcting your mistakes
● hang on to the positive
● release the negative.

Could you allocate some time each day as this top achiever does? Could you write down the positive? What steps can you take? Think about it as you read the next paragraphs.

Eliminate the doldrums

The best way to eliminate the doldrums is to take a moment to acknowledge your strengths and what you do right. Take time to acknowledge your persistence, your stamina, your determination, your progress in being organized, your sales skill building and so on.

Watch children as a clue to human development. A two-year-old says, 'I can do it, I can do it, I can do it.' A three-year-old says, 'I did it, I did it, I did it.' They go from conviction, determination and belief to success.

That's what we need to do too in creating success patterns. First, we have to have a positive attitude about the fact that we *can* do it, and then we have to reinforce the fact that we have done it.

That's the reason you have to stop to give yourself acknowledgement for your progress and success. Don't wait until you reach the end result because you'll get into the doldrums waiting. Acknowledge yourself for the small steps along the way.

 For maximum success, write down your success steps and review them every evening or when you're most likely to get the doldrums.

Most people find it easier to criticize themselves than to acknowledge themselves. It comes from years of incorrect practice. Now is the time to reverse the process. When you acknowledge yourself, your morale will go up. And high morale is essential to keeping yourself going.

Your skills and qualities

Make a list now of skills and qualities you can acknowledge in yourself. Then you'll be able to refer to these when you need a morale boost.

Dare to be different

Another top sales executive hired a secretary after being in insurance for only six months. No one else was willing to be so daring and invest in themselves *before* their income was high. But he saw the potential of doing what he did best and delegating everything else. Now he has four members on his support staff and *ten times* the average income!

The chances are that you're holding yourself back from something. It may be hiring an assistant or trying a new method no one else uses. It might be investing in equipment or support staff, or doing presentations or demos a different way. Whatever it is, look again. Think again. Don't be afraid to be different.

Perhaps you will be an inspiration, not only for yourself but for others. There are plenty of mediocre salespeople doing things in their standard way, getting standard results. If you want to be successful, you have to be determined, committed, positive, disciplined and different.

Being different alone won't do it. But being different on top of being determined, committed, positive and disciplined can put you on a new level. What are you holding yourself back from? Now decide what you are willing to do about it. Focus on the long-term effect you'll create and not the short-term resistance to change you may get from those around you.

Make a list like this and jot down your answers.

What am I holding myself back from?	
What am I willing to do about it?	
What result could I expect?	

Overcome roadblocks

Most people see a number of roadblocks between themselves and their goal. Roadblocks always exist.

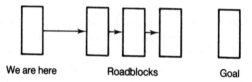

The mentality shift that helps us overcome roadblocks is totally straightforward: keep the goal in sight and focus determinedly on ways around the roadblocks. It looks like this:

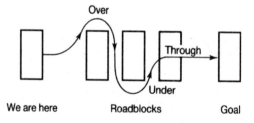

In reality, roadblocks are nothing more than challenges that help us grow. One person's roadblock is nothing to another person because they've already gained skills in that direction. So why not go in that direction to gain those skills as well?

Move quickly to your goal

Let's ask ourselves these questions:

● What happens if we have no goal?
● What if our goal isn't clear in our mind?
● What if we see our goal as one big chunk rather than daily pieces?

We may feel that we're moving too slowly or not at all towards our goal. We get caught in a downward spiral.

What can we do every day to make sure we're creating an upward spiral, moving closer to our goal? The answer is to have our goal clearly defined, break it into action segments, and tackle the segments every day without fail.

> **'Happiness is directly proportional to the speed you're moving towards your goal.'**

When you develop that discipline, success will be in your hands. Without it, you're giving your power away. What is *your* clearly defined goal? What are the segments that will help you reach it?

Take the most challenging path

One successful woman I know says, 'When you come to a crossroad in life, take the most challenging path.' Why does she advocate this? Because challenges make us grow and make us feel good about ourselves. If we turn away from the challenging path, we stagnate.

I talked about this concept in a speech to a group of sales executives in Malaysia, among whom was an IBM salesman. A year and a half later, he came to me and said that this advice had completely changed his life. He had been doing well already but, with his new determination to take the most challenging paths at every turn, his life had become incredibly rich with new and exciting opportunities.

Think now of what challenging paths lie before you. Perhaps you haven't seen them in this light before. Perhaps they would also bring you rich, new and exciting opportunities. It's important not to turn your back on them. Having the courage to take the challenging path and overcome the roadblocks requires conviction that we'll succeed. The best way to do this is to harness strength from past successes.

Think first of what roadblocks you perceive to be in front of you, standing in the way of your challenging path.

Consider your past successes

Think now of all your past successes. Think of your successes early in your career, early in your education. Think of any contest or competition you won, no matter how young you were. What quality did you have which helped you win? You still have it. Now is the time to harness this to help you overcome your roadblocks.

Every individual has a great deal more potential than they ever imagine. The goal or vision you have in your mind must be exactly right for you because no one else has that same vision. Don't let a simple roadblock stop you. Use your strengths to overcome it.

Summary

Today we studied the most important factors for implementing motivation and support systems.

We saw that being in sales is much like running our own business. Our remuneration, or some of it, is often linked to our results. No sales = no pay. Thus we need to be our own coach, our own cheerleader, our own goal setter and our own creator of a structure for working that brings us success.

We also analysed the steps of the sales process that require the most support, and looked at ways we can get that support. We learned how to stay positive when the going gets tough, how to release negativity and how to eliminate the doldrums and self-criticism. We looked at why we might dare to be different or to take the most challenging path. And, most of all, we looked at the over-under-through method of overcoming obstacles, which can be used not only in sales but also in all aspects of life.

Remember

When you come to a crossroad in life, take the most challenging path.

SUNDAY

MONDAY

TUESDAY

WEDNESDAY

THURSDAY

FRIDAY

SATURDAY

Fact-check (answers at the back)

1. What's the key to getting support from people?
   a) Being willing to give them reciprocal support ❏
   b) Deciding what kind of support you want and asking for it specifically ❏
   c) Setting your goals, and sharing your progress ❏
   d) All of the above ❏

2. What is the first step to staying positive?
   a) Noticing your thoughts ❏
   b) Eating a good breakfast ❏
   c) Working out every day ❏
   d) Meeting with your boss in the morning ❏

3. What is the best way to eliminate the doldrums?
   a) Taking time to acknowledge what you do right ❏
   b) Taking time to acknowledge your persistence ❏
   c) Acknowledging your determination ❏
   d) All of the above ❏

4. What's important about keeping your morale high with regard to increasing your sales?
   a) People will like you ❏
   b) It keeps you going ❏
   c) Your family will notice ❏
   d) You'll feel good about yourself ❏

5. What's the most important step in creating success patterns?
   a) Know what you want to do ❏
   b) Get permission from your boss ❏
   c) Have a positive attitude that you can do it ❏
   d) Write down your plan ❏

6. Why should you not wait until you reach your goal to acknowledge yourself, but instead acknowledge your progress along the way?
   a) To help you remember where you are going ❏
   b) To help you remember why you are going there ❏
   c) Because it's too long to wait until the end ❏
   d) To stay out of the doldrums and keep motivation high ❏

7. Why do most people find it easier to criticize themselves than to acknowledge themselves?
   a) Other people like it ❏
   b) They learned it in childhood ❏
   c) They've had years of practice ❏
   d) It feels right ❏

8. Why is it good to make a list of your skills and qualities and refer to it occasionally?
   a) It brings a smile to your face ❏
   b) You get good ideas from referring to it ❏
   c) It boosts your morale ❏
   d) It helps you defend your position when you need to ❏

9. What's a good way to get around roadblocks?
a) Think of them as nothing more than challenges that help us grow ❏
b) Go around them: over, under or through ❏
c) Stop and do something else ❏
d) Both a and b ❏

10. What's good about the following philosophy? 'When you come to a crossroad in life, take the most challenging path.'
a) Challenges make us grow ❏
b) It gives you more exercise ❏
c) If we turn away from the most challenging path, we stagnate ❏
d) Both a and c ❏

Surviving in tough times

No one likes tough times. It brings fear to the marketplace. Employers don't know if their customers will survive, or even if their suppliers will survive. The great news, however, is that there is never more demand for good salespeople than in tough economic times. Armed with the skills described in these seven chapters, you'll have the confidence and ability to find a rewarding, highly paid sales position.

Here are ten crucial tips to help you achieve that goal and make a big impact on your career.

1 Talk about targets

Whether you are looking for a better job, seeking a promotion or aiming for a pay rise, remember that *everyone* responds well to the concept of targets. When selling to a customer, talk to them about *their* targets. This shows them that you care and that you understand the challenges they face. Then, let them know how your product or service can help them reach *their* targets.

Let prospective employers hear you talk targets, targets, targets. This will tell them that you have systems that guarantee you will reach *their* targets. By talking about targets, you'll be talking their language! And don't forget to dwell on your own targets daily to maximize your success.

2 Visit current and past customers

Some salespeople avoid speaking with current and past clients, fearing that they might get complaints. Actually, the opposite is true. By interviewing past and current clients about the benefits they've derived from your product or service, you're likely to reinvigorate their interest and commitment. You're likely to pique their interest in other products and services you offer, leading to new sales. And in the process, you're likely to gain three valuable benefits for yourself: product knowledge, testimonials and referrals.

3 Understand buying motives

As many as 80 per cent of unsuccessful salespeople try to sell their product or service before they know the buying motives of the customer. They assume they know the motive but, as with anything in life, assumptions are often wrong. If you want to maximize your closings, you need to ask your prospect about the benefits and features they require. By doing this, you'll be able to zero in on their exact needs with your presentation. You'll save countless hours, which you'll be able to use to close more sales. You'll have time left over for more prospecting and you'll join the top 20 per cent of sales professionals.

4 Assume flexibility

An intriguing aspect of human nature is its flexibility. Customers often start out thinking that they must have features A, B and C in a product or service. However, when presented with X, Y and Z, they often become fascinated and shift their priorities. The lesson of this is simple: to maximize sales, don't be discouraged when you don't have all the features the customer first asks for. Other aspects of your product or service may satisfy or override those being initially sought. They may have more faith in you and your company than in your competitor. By exploring these concepts rather than settling for defeat, you will prosper.

5 Turn objections to your advantage

Objections never stop the top 2 per cent of sales professionals. In fact, they treasure objections. To join their ranks and learn to value objections, you need to understand that prospective customers are showing interest when they bring up objections. If a person has no interest, they won't waste time bringing up objections. The top 2 per cent choose to see the objection as a question, as an encouragement. Then they proceed with the three-part process shown in Wednesday's chapter. By adopting this attitude and skill yourself, you will join the top 2 per cent, and you'll not only survive in tough times, you'll also gain enormously.

6 Master the component parts

Successful selling is not a fly-by-the-seat-of-the-pants process. A successful sales process has a precise structure. Learn that structure and you'll succeed. Just as in the manufacturing process, there are component parts in the sales process, which include discovering the corporate and personal buying motive, gaining product expertise, knowing your competitors' strengths and weaknesses, linking needs to benefits, overcoming objections, reviewing their needs and the benefits we offer and – last, but not least – the successful close. By mastering these, you'll turn tough times into good times, possibly the best ever.

7 Strike while the iron is hot

Fewer than 20 per cent of salespeople maximize the closing of sales, because they miss the right time to ask for the business. After putting tremendous effort into prospecting, setting up appointments and making presentations, ineffective salespeople walk away from the business by not asking timely closing questions. They fool themselves into thinking that they don't need to ask for the business, or they wait too long. Don't let this happen to you. Study the 'customer interest cycle' in Friday's chapter and master 'striking while the iron is hot'.

8 Create your own action-provoking system

In order to survive in tough times, we need to make each minute count – be it in closing a sale or gaining more prospects. The best way to do this is to create a foolproof, easy-to-use system that will tell you which prospect needs to be closed each day, as well as how many new prospects need to be acquired. Friday's chapter gives you tried and true methods for creating a system perfect for you, that will allow you to know instantly where to put your efforts each day to maximize your sales.

9 Dare to be different

To succeed at the highest levels in sales, think of yourself as running your own business. If you owned a retail or a manufacturing business, you would undoubtedly run it according to your own judgement. You wouldn't follow the practices of other business owners, especially if they were unsuccessful or mediocre in their results. However, when salespeople have good ideas about how to run their sales practice but see no one else doing it, they often hold themselves back. Don't let this happen to you. To turn tough times into prosperous times, follow your inspiration and dare to be different.

10 Take the most challenging path

When you come to a crossroad in life, you have two choices. You can take the easy road, the familiar one that you've travelled before. Alternatively, you can take the more challenging road, the one you've not tried before. The choice is yours.

Research shows that the most successful people choose the challenging path. They do this because it offers personal growth, variety and a chance to use and improve their skills and knowledge. This leads to higher responsibility, higher income, and high satisfaction. The next time you're faced with a decision, think about taking the most challenging path in order to survive and prosper in tough times.

Answers

Sunday: 1d; 2d; 3b; 4c; 5b; 6d; 7a; 8c; 9d; 10b.

Monday: 1c; 2a; 3c; 4d; 5d; 6a; 7d; 8b; 9d; 10d.

Tuesday: 1d; 2a; 3b; 4a; 5c; 6d; 7d; 8d; 9b; 10b.

Wednesday: 1d; 2c; 3a; 4d; 5d; 6d; 7a; 8b; 9b; 10d.

Thursday: 1d; 2a; 3d; 4a; 5b; 6d; 7d; 8b; 9b; 10c.

Friday: 1b; 2b; 3d; 4d; 5d; 6d; 7a; 8d; 9d; 10d.

Saturday: 1d; 2a; 3d; 4b; 5c; 6d; 7c; 8c; 9d; 10d.

Notes

ALSO AVAILABLE IN THE 'IN A WEEK' SERIES

For information about other titles in the series, please visit
www.inaweek.co.uk

ALSO AVAILABLE IN THE 'IN A WEEK' SERIES

For information about other titles
in the series, please visit
www.inaweek.co.uk